ADEOLU EMMANUEL ADESANYA

WHY *Ask* WHY

A collection of poems

author**HOUSE®**

AuthorHouse™ UK
1663 Liberty Drive
Bloomington, IN 47403 USA
www.authorhouse.co.uk
Phone: 0800.197.4150

Published by AuthorHouse   12/10/2014

ISBN: 978-1-4969-9835-4 (sc)
ISBN: 978-1-4969-9836-1 (e)

Contents

To my son
Ololade Gideon Adesanya

And my daughter
Ifeoluwa Praise Adesanya

Acknowledgements

All glory, praise and adoration to God almighty - the giver of life, wisdom and inspiration.

Special thank you to my parents Ven. Dr. Stephen A. Adesanya and Mrs Ololade O. Adesanya; to my wife Kehinde O. Adesanya; my children Ololade and Ifeoluwa Adesanya; and my brother Adedotun S. Adesanya, for their support, encouragement, prayer, patience and love.

If only the world were full of the likes of Leah Godson, my efficacious editor for her selflessness, dedication, mentoring, and words of encouragement. You are a rare gem.

To my friends and muses; Ayodele Alonge, Oluwaseun Liadi, Jessica Movilau, Emmanuel Ashiabor, Ayisat Hammed, Fatuma Mishi, Wale Ogunnowo, thank you for being there to share my laughter and tears. To Maj. Gen. T.B and Mrs. Ogundeko, Ms Nike Okunowo, Mrs Edith Eneaya-Bonito, Barr. Kunle Daodu, Engr. Babafemi Osoba DIG (Rtd), thank you for your consistent love and dedication.

To poets near and far, Words Rhyme and Rhythm, London Poets Meet up, and various social media poetry groups, thank you for the learning experience.

Why Ask Why?

When heaven opens and won't stop
All washed away but our tears
When life ends before it even begins
When we ask, yet no response
To why God stopped loving us

When earth opens and all caves in
All we hold dear now but a dream
When the children look so old
And they ask you for their family
Do you say God hated them that much?

When the ground vibrates and all crashes
Hope fades before it even starts
When air and wind churn
And there's nowhere to turn but inward
To all prayers, did He stop listening?

When loved ones passes on
Leaving you clutching memories
No one to face, as no one faces you
Heart too heavy to carry
As you ask God "why me?"

Mountains melt, my mind freezes
Rocks crash; ashes on my head
Landslides, ghosts come visiting
The walls come closing in
And we ask why He made us

His way so mysterious, not ours
His reason, the wise can't comprehend
Our pains and tears, He sees
For He felt it first, so is love.

2.

Motherly Tree on Earth

I hear your dirge, all night long
Singing unending, the same sad song
No one listens to you, because no one cares
But I do know your pain, and the burden you bare.

Through rain and sun, you stand still tall
With your head raised high, we scarcely see it fall
Yours is not pride, when you spread out your arms
It is to give, though you receive no alms.

You have no place to rest, to lay your weary head
Yet many abodes you provide, to nest the birds
You stand there alone, no one to lean on
Yet on you we climb, scale, swing and cling on.

Yours is a life of persecution, yet you persevere
Rather than shed tears, you shed leaves
And if they cut your branches so that you won't spread
Your roots go deep and widen instead.

You ride the storms, and withstand the seasons
You could have run, but you stayed, for many reasons
Let the rain whip, let the sun heat, like a burner
They simply make you bigger, stronger, and taller.

3.

Remilekun

Angelic face in place
She makes them fall
A demonic shape in shades
She called them Saul
Don't blow her whistle
Else you dance to her tune

She whipped the crack
Her slaves in sweet bondage
She blinked but once
Their hearts skipped twice
And to her great designs
They're duty bound

You hate to love her
But her web she spins
Just like a spider
You're the croaking frog
Don't receive her kiss
Else you become her prince

An enigma plus one
A beauty plus fun
A temptress in eon
She laughs in turn
But when she's done
You're hooked and gone.

Road of Life

Addie, did you see that road ahead?
Not the sandy one
That violently sprays dust at passers-by,
That makes clean cars shudder with fright
Or drivers lungs recoil in horror,
No, not that road.
For that road is not your path
Too perfect for a man like you

Don't turn into the left road either
No, I know it's not pleasant
The mud and filthy water
Slippery path and hidden potholes
That turn high heels to statues
A nightmare for white garments
No, not that road
It might fit your personality
But it's too good to be true for you.

Oh no, not the road to the right
So tempting to walk down
Bar the dangerous curves and turf
Highway to heaven and hell
A one way ticket, no return
With blood and bones sprawled over
Smeared across in pints, not drops
That could easily be your lot!!!
But then again, why settle for less?

Don't be tempted to turn back
You're thinking, could it be any worse
At least that road, you've taken once
Hard and treacherous, I know.
Yet familiar evil, familiar neighbour
But it's too late and you've clocked out
And in case you're wishing for a second chance
That is unaffordable luxury.

But if you can't go ahead or back
Turn to the left or right
Being stagnant is not an option
You can either sink or fly away
Addie, you may not be worthy enough
To take any of these roads
Or maybe, just maybe you're too good
And destined to fly and soar away.

5.

Colour Me Blind

The lies that we tell have lives of their own
And each day we live a lie
We just want to make things lie low
Never for the truth to surface
Else words will crumble like cornflakes
As we simply don't want to lose face

We'd rather stick it in a hole
Wishing things would just fly past
Like the villains that just were
We tell the story just like it was
Except the story just wasn't like that
Editing and twisting
We alter and flip the story
Upside down and inside out
And my life, I barely know
And myself, I scarcely hear
As the story just won't add up
As I'm reading someone else's script
When it comes out, it doesn't sound right
As my corrupted mind doesn't feel right
As this just simply isn't right
It knows when all else turns left, I must turn right
And my dire need to make things right
And set off the light in this fight
Else I might just end up in this shite
And sink so deep that I've lost my sight
And things that matters most I barely see

Because the truth and lies,
and lies and truth are one and the same
And the more that I search, the more I'm confused
And like rays of colours, all set to dazzle, leaving me to marvel
They colour me blind.

We're like two kids in the same place
Looking and seeing the same things
From the same angle, at the same time
Yet you call it black, I call it white
Even if our sight is paired in
Black and White.
This is looking more like the same old joke
Please don't call it colour blindness
Is grey the same as silver?
Or dust mistaken for ashes
If it's the truth am telling
Why does my heart say I'm lying
I feel just as it comes out
That it's all doctored throughout
And no amount of gagging
Can alter the words from the altar
The lightening of thunder
The magic of a rainbow
My mirror asunder
And the tilt of your bow are but
Gimmicks of your deception
To colour me blind.

6.

My Pain, Your Gain

I'm loud, but I'm not a tout!
I'm not a clown although I shout!!
Don't grade me because I'm in rage,
As being deranged is not being displaced.
My pain might be your gain
but don't blink, as it might be you again,
as fate may reverse the role
and in my life, you play the lead role.
It is dark, but will you walk the road?
Crushing weight, can you carry the load?
So, stop pretending you know me
and think twice before you judge me,
as what you see is what I show you,
a tiny fragment of my reality and
a clouded part of your imagination.
And what you know of me today
defines what you know of yourself,
as parameters employed in judging me:
replicate your abstract wealth;
the volume of your worth; and
the quality of your personality.
Hence until you feel the depth of my pain;
get quenched by the same icy rain;
whipped with ache like that of Cain;
and walk my path taking same stony lane,
Don't sit there on your mighty horse
calling me a tout because am loud,
or a clown because I shout.
My pain might be your gain,
but then, it might be you again.

7.

Son of a Preacher

Right from childhood,
I knew no other way.
Right from wrong,
I was shown all the way.
The path of being righteous,
all straight and narrow;
No beast, flesh or foe
can shoot me an arrow,
As all days geared towards one,
the glory of the former
can't compare to the last one.
In my own rights, I'm a special one:

the son of a preacher,
and God's specially chosen one.
Hence my scale like no other -
The epitome of all goodness,
The standard to measure all moral.
My hands, head and heart,
a tool shortlisted by grace and favour,
Emancipated from former self in
Glorification of His holy name.

8.

I Love Dead People

Don't stand near a bucket
As you might unwittingly kick it
Don't put the blade in your pocket
As it might end up in your heart
In our preoccupation to make a hit
We usually ends up hitting wrong targets
The victim, being ourselves first
Then our very best friend next
While his, might be a death sentence
Yours is life, strewn in vile sentences.

Yeah, keep puffing the black smoke
Lining white powder in strokes
Getting high and lost in coke
Till you start seeing dead folk
Then you gasp like you're in a head choke
Panting like you're having a stroke
Working towards the next fix is a yoke
The brunt of it all because you're the joke.
You walk dead, think dead, look dead
And the last to know that you are dead.

You sell your soul on a guilt trip
You're loved by all is a good trick
Think you're ageless like an oak tree
Walking high on a cloud trails
Paying by blood like it's a good treat
You love fast life but it's too fast
All fast forwarded to your demise
You have it all, but you miss a bit
Li'l laughter, l'il tears, l'il love, l'il fear
And that's because you're a dead man.

9.

Nothingness

The first shrill cry of a new baby
The last heaving sigh of a dying body
The beginning and end of nothingness
From the exasperation of morning dew
To the desperation that was overdue
From the quest to amass all
Whilst toiling from nothingness
To the realisation that amazes none
That once gone, finder's kept.
And it all start all over again
The strife and pursuit of vanity.

10.

Not My Friend

As the tears drop his grin widens
As they flow he breaks into a smile
He causes the unfortunate event
He performs the nefarious activity
While I face the painful consequences
My friend indeed.

He counts all I do wrong and ignores all I do right
All but he see my excellent actions
This cynic claims to be my best friend
But he stabs my deepest wound
Through him my secrets are unveiled
My friend indeed.

In my presence, his praise for me knows no bounds
But crucifixion starts once my back is turned
He salivates when I am loaded
But on the opposite coast he stands when I'm broke
He disappears mysteriously when I'm in need
Yet he claims to be my friend indeed.

Never shall you be my friend
You who never see my good deed
You who never rebuke me in my presence
You who never praise me in my absence
A friend in need is a friend indeed
You are not my friend.

11.

What if I Was?

A couple of sleepless nights
And the same familiar stranger
Metamorphoses into an evolution
She's heavy in agony
Scales over the nine walls
And then comes the shrill cry
What if I was born?

Like a blurred vision
The natal season changes rapidly
From the attachment of a name
'Till its confirmation by the bearer
The transformation in heart, head and hands
From unsteady totter to majestic walk
I sojourn into the unknown
What if I was growing?

The independent becomes responsible
Commitment mounts on appointment
Life soaked in panic and in the fear
Of retrenchment and unemployment
More mouths to feed than hand can meet
The predicament of the breadwinner
Sleeping with one eye open
Living to work and not vice-versa
What if I was working?

Two legs turn three overnight
Black mane turns grey then white
Gums let go of teeth
Ailments come calling
The mind fails under frequent tests
Composing its memoir
Only to forget it immediately
Sleeping, but appearing dead
What if I had died?

12.

Our Flower

We both see it together
Though I see it before you
Yet you see it coming.
We both arrive at its base
And reach the resolution
To tender and nurture it
In togetherness, our flower.

I prune, tend and protect it
You water it tenderly
You make sure it has sunlight
I make sure it never gets
Dry and withered.
In this union of togetherness
Our flower grows up rapidly.

Then comes the wind, a whirlwind
Shaking it to the base
Then comes the rain, with its companion
A terrifying storm that erodes.
The sudden and unpredicted change
Makes us lose the passion and commitment
And our flower suffers exceedingly.

The cracks show in its ever-solid ground
The ever-radiant leaves change colour
Its ever-amazing stature loses balance
Yet its fruit is just around the corner.
Please come back my love
And share with me the fruit
Of our togetherness, our flower.

13.

Foolish Magician

Lights beams then fizzles out like a mirage
With convincing acts full of suspense
Rushing as if in a blinding rage
That goes anti- clockwise, then malfunction.

He's a magician, but foolish are his ways
He brings tears and laughter, the village idiot
A friend best kept far, feeble minds, dodgy ways
Hanging upside down, his neck too close to the noose.

He knows no shame, takes pride in his spoils
So brief an encounter, that's all that matters
A game to win, a heart to break
Sprinkling dust as glitters, and believing his lies.

He cuts them loose, they're dispersed garbage
No backward glance, it's time for a new adventure
A thirst for new blood, a dire need for carnage
Magic and folly, a heart in chains for torture.

14.

When God is in it

When God is in it
It's a burden being lifted
Feeling joy like a river in my soul
Living my life anew
It's a new dawn, a new day.

It's a new dawn, a new day
Living my life anew
Feeling joy like a river in my soul
It's a burden being lifted
When God is in it.

15.

God, Give Me an Amen

Innermost yearning, heart craving
As I star gaze, my limbs stretching
Mighty aspirations as I lay daydreaming
For a better tomorrow
Starting from today, so shall it be.

For the tears that startle my eyes
For the dark shadows that won't bulge
even as I glimpse on the horizon, my sun
For the grace to kneel, the courage to ask
For a new day, a new me
And so shall it be, Amen.

A new song to sing, a spring in my step
The days of the dirge remain in the past
To be birthed forth a lion
from the carcass of an ant
Who strides in grace amazing
When the heaven echo Amen.

To dance in the music of a thunder clap
To shine in the glory of a wintery sun
To praise in victory of tomorrow's battle
With music of a thousand bands
For these, and much more
God, give me an Amen.

An Amen for each day and hour
To see deeper even when in the deep
To take fall-backs, as a catapult being launched.
And when my mind argues with your promises
To have the will to scream in sheer ecstasy
"Your words are ye, and Amen."

16.

Bring Back our Girls

"Bring back our girls."
From the darkest pit comes the ghoulish wail,
Stolen futures in blood and in years.

Their voices rummage through the jungle and bounce off trees
Soulless, masked in blood-stained gear, they muster their call.
"Bring back our girls."

They ought to know better, do better, our clueless leaders,
who hide away in rocks built like high walls,
Stealing futures in blood and in years.

Parents try in vain to wipe away their tears;
they dare not grieve; perplexed they yell
"bring back our girls."

Their safety was assured and the girls believed their lies,
But into the unknown they sojourned through hell,
Stolen futures in blood and in years.

The long dark night is almost over, Chibok girls;
Run nigh and walk tall but do not fall.
"Bring back our girls."
Stolen futures in blood and in years.

17.

My Voice

Mine is a voice that won't be still, it won't shush.
It set its own path, creating its own niche
Loud or low, it stirs and spurs; it won't take "no."
Or else I'll be boiling; a fiery volcano
That cascades the height, to build or crush.

A voice that can't be bought, don't evaluate
It re-echoes truth, it resonates
It stares at injustice till it cowers
and obliterates it like it ne'er was
It hammers, crushing and melting evil's gate.

A voice that can't be erased as it's published;
It sinks into the mind and is firmly established.
Spearing guilty hearts and salting sores
as it redresses societal ills and its gores
until slates are made cleaned and left polished.

18.

She's One of a Kind

When I say she's one of a kind,
being merely different doesn't cut the contrast
that's glaring when in comparison with others of her kind.

It goes much deeper and further
than you can give a definite meaning to
so complex, yet so simple in her kind of way.

Someone asked, does that mean she's a kind person?
Her unique kindness is the start of grasping and delving
into the profound depth of her personality,
unequal in all kinds of ways, making her a one of a kind.

The kind of person that can go all the way to heaven and back
to bring you answered prayers,
and simultaneously journey to hell and back to fight your corner,
and that makes her one of a kind.

Her touch is like being pelted with tender roses,
her hugs rival the warmth of an angel's wing,
her smile is enough to melt all the ice in the North Pole;
yes go ahead and blame her for global warming,
she's one of a kind who's got enough warmth
to make the world glow with joy

She's the kind of person that freezes time when you're in her company,
yet you can't seem to have enough,
she's surely a special one,
my special one, my one of a kind.

19.

Not by Fate, but by Faith

My spirit dwells in You, lest any sorrow rise
From ruminating on timorous snapshots of yesteryears
Hence, my inner sight have I set on Your Word
Humans interpret through eyes, but You through my heart.

My feet have I stilted with His omnipresence.
Though my ways are not His, neither my thoughts.
Yet I walk with Him whom I see not, but who sees me.
Therefore my walk is not by fate, but by faith.

I meditate on Your ordinances, not worldly news
That's full of woe and gore, bile and lies
And my cares and worries have I cast on You
Of good report am I, an over-conqueror.

Not worried about what to eat, to drink, to wear.
For I am but a priority in His grandeur
And if birds are singing, flowers are clothed in grandeur
Then my tomorrow, through faith, is grand.

20.

The Man in the Bowler Hat

In a bowler hat away he goes
A sheepish grin plastered on his face
Head tilted to ease the sweat
With each step, the longer his shadow.

Legs of steel but heart of mush
His pace light and brisk
His face conceals his true urgency
Hastening towards the bank at high tide.

You see the grin wearing thin
As he navigates the beach
His shadow darkens and shortens
In his reminiscence that defines all.

He assumes serene calmness on arrival
To get his mission underway
A glance darted either way is all he needs -
The go ahead signal to take a deep breath.

You sense the air heavy from his stoic look
The breeze a freezing wreck
The sea frightfully nervous
As waves clash one against the other.

He heaves and up he goes
Like a limp sack, he nosedives
A quick spasm of water, and all is calm
But for the bowler hat floating away.

I Did it My own way

I want to see the world with my own eyes
Capture life in frames with my own lens
But you reckon I could do better, using yours
Aged with life lessons and experience

I want to walk and make my own path
Go far and near, till I find my own pace
To you, I'm a fool going where angels fear to tread
But let it be known, I walked my own way

I want to hear, make up my own mind
Be a man, form and live by my own words
Here's yours, you've ever been so kind
And if mine falters, let it be my own fault.

I want to climb, I want to fly
Perilous high, hovering on clouds
And if I fall flat on my face, to you, I won't cry
I'll pick myself up, try all over again.

I want to live life my own way
Love and hate based on how I feel
Laugh or weep, let it be done my own way
And at the end to say, "I did it my own way".

22.

Dark Clouds

Brush swivelling furiously as it burrows
Wielded by weird artist with dark colours
Clothed gothic, I'm the canvass
Left transparent for the downfall

My heart in hands to collect
Every dripping, shedding and pouring
Don't add the bleeding and the tears
That got mixed up with the rainfall

It crashes as the thunder clashes
My mind muffles momentarily in time
Scary and jittery even my own shadow
Abandons me as the night falls

Like a whirlwind spiralling out of synch
I feel all spinning out of check
My lot cast on a roller coaster ride
Towards its final destination at skyfall

It's scary dark, but I will find a way
Blinded by my tears, I will surely see
Amidst the noise, I will hear your voice
Guiding me to a place of bliss, a waterfall.

23.

Aroma of Love and Lust

Every minute spent with you pulls me an inch nearer
The truth in your eyes, hypnotising my heart deeper
The warmth of your embrace arrests my soul, rendering me
A captive of emotions, engulfed in wild flame.

I crave your poison, my guilty pleasure
Surrender to your wile, and your savage torture
Yearning in sweet surrender for your angelic touch
That sends my heart pulsating in an unending crush

My heart the pendulum, can't stop from swinging
From lusting after you, to loving and falling for you.
Strong the aroma, your scented courses
But my mind is in denial, starving my senses.

24.

Like a Flower

Like a flower it opens
All it needs is a little warmth
To make it bloom
A little moisture
To bring it to life
And a little love
To make it grow
Deep and wide
Big and strong

Like a flower, it's beautiful
Shaped like a heart
To draw you
Scented sweet by nature
To attract you
Dripping juice like nectar
To touch your senses
And it's taste
Magical and addictive
Just like a flower.

Like a flower it germinates
When planted
Takes patience to grow
Takes long to mature
When flowering
Takes so much effort to nurture
But when it's fully ripen
It grows with grace as it ages
Just like a flower.

Except it's not a flower
It doesn't come
With the many shapes of a flower
It doesn't come
With its array of enchanting colours
It doesn't come
With the immobile nature of a flower
But when it comes
It comes strong, fast and sharp
It makes all flowers go grey with envy.

25.

Don't Break My Heart

If these floodgates are opened,
They won't stop till they drown you
So don't break my heart, my love
Else my tears will gush, like a flood.

If this cannon is let loose
It won't stop till it wrecks you
So don't break my heart, my love
Else my voice will destroy, like a tornado.

If these waves come crashing down
They won't stop till they submerge you
So don't break my heart, my love
Else my arms won't embrace, but smother.

So don't go breaking my heart
It is fragile, so handle with care
But also volatile, a raging storm
It can love endlessly, or wage war ferociously.

26.

Poetic Gospel

Particles of norms coming down in forms
Abstract ideas popping up like lumps
Some need scrapping, others simply give a slap
A eureka moment when I open the poetic tap.

Some words seep through the veins to make the grade
Some are squeezed in vain, ends losing out in the trade
Bubbles of words popping through my pen
Or babbles that make perfect sense for my poem

The niggling urge to scribble whilst blazing hot
And to stir words as they sizzle in my poetic pot
I'll make up the ingredients along my new path
Then have a taste, maybe share, in part.

The silence of day screaming for my attention
Or the chaos of mind-set urging me to take caution
Either way, my emotions supersede to form the theme
And words simply leap out to dance to the rhythm.

27.

Guilty Conscience

One minute laughing, the next crying
The crease of your smile turning down to a frown
You reveal your real self as my face is turned
Faking that smile and stifling that sob.

You've got it on, your concealing mask
To shield me from seeing, from knowing
But no matter how hard you try, you can't
A star can't hide away from the moon.

I see the truth and its pain in your eyes,
I hear the crack and quiver in your voice
I feel the murmur as your heart bleeds
I am your true soul, your conscience

Let go of the floodgate, let it cleanse
Purge away the lies and the shame
Soon the twinkle shall be seen in your eyes again
And no guilt will muffle the laughter in your soul.

28.

God, Show Me You're there with Me

When the wind of life blows hard
And I'm engulfed in gusts of hot air
When chaos and whirlwinds billow
God, show me You're there with me
And let me feel Your breath of life.

When fire of life burns high
And sparks of pressure ignite
When scared and scarred by burns
God, show me you're there with me
And let me feel the warmth of Your love.

When I'm stuck in the pit of life
Covered in its dust, dirt, and grime
When stranded and swamped in quicksand
God, show me You're there with me
And let me feel Your powerful pull.

When I'm swayed by the storms of life
Bewildered by its hailstorms and hurricanes
When all roads seem neither right nor wrong
God, show me You're there with me
And let me feel Your leading presence.

29.

A Man Like that

I've got it bottled up
A man of few words
Let my actions speak for themselves
My face, sometimes like a puzzle
As I'm a man like that

I've got it all contained
My emotions and fears
A man must never cry
Hence, the water seeps out not as tears but as
My hot, manly sweat

I've got it all covered
My thoughts and feelings
A man never speaks out of turn
But push too far, and watch me roar
In my baritone manly voice

I've got it locked away
Its key, hidden in the secret bay
Not my skeletons, but my heart
And if you unearth and unlock it
Do not break it, but love it.

30.

Cursed Blessing
– Malachi 2:2

It started off like manna from heaven
Self-centred, you cramped all, into your haven
Your gluttony led to indigestion
Now you're now drowning in your overflowing.

You prayed and fasted for a job
He answered; now you work till you're numb
Schedule full, too busy now to pray
In pain, all your salary turns to drugs' prey.

In blessing, I will bless thee
But if it will take you away from Me
Then, I will curse all your blessings
Just like a prodigal, till you learn your lessons.

31.

God at Work

The serene atmosphere attests to the Almighty planning out His day
The firmament in its multi-layers echoes the complexity
Sometimes He add a few clouds for good measure
Some fill the air with humidity, joining us for company
Or the overzealous sun in search for extra brownie points
Some spill their emotions in tears, the ground floods in delight
As it cheer us on walking on waters - us little gods.
Whilst His glory glistens like a crown endowed with diamonds
Emphasising how on a daily basis, He made us priority.

32.

My Love for You

My love for you is like
The burning sun in the Sahara
It ostentatiously warms the day
And tenaciously tends its path
Till it bids a wistful farewell at dusk.

My love for you is like
The River Nile in its elongated flow
Coming from a source, so deep and pure
It transcends others in tireless vigour
Trailing you, wave after wave in bliss.

My love for you is like
The tall towering Iroko tree
It conquers all in conquest for you
Shields and protects in adversity
A strong and reliable wall to lean on.

My love for you is like
The dark loamy soil in the Savannah
A fertile platform for you to grow on
It nurtures and pampers
Till you yield bountifully in goodness.

Yes you, my African jewel
My love for you is like
Your ample Afro hair
Beautifying; an object of pride
To behold, to love, and to complete.

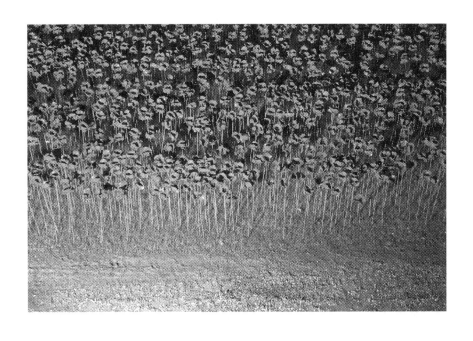

33.

We Will Remember

Those that fell on the roadside
Those buried alive in the trenches
The lost souls on the war front
We'll never forget, we will remember

The old and infirm, who went anyway
Those too young, who added years overnight
For the women out there with them, to care
We'll never forget, we will remember.

The child waiting fora father that will never come home
The wife waiting for a husband that's been lost to war
The parents waiting for their fallen son
We'll never forget, we will remember

The millions of souls lost to war
The millions maimed for life
The millions who'll never recover their losses
We'll never forget, we will remember

The politicians who were right about the war
The masses who were left after
All your sacrifices, your many losses
We'll never forget, we will remember.

34.

Figurine's World

A gap to fill, a need to meet
A life with a mind in turmoil
Purpose a mush, routine a bore
For a dreamer who wobbles on a tightrope

Time ticking, game almost over
Failure stares at tragicomedy
Heart in pieces, dreams in false aura
Fleecing hope chasing shadowy honey

Tears to wipe, lies to unsay,
Lost in trance as she slips through the cracks
Echoes of guilt, pangs of defeat
A kite cut loose in the turbulent wind

Fading yesteryears, lavished glories
Routine a pendulum in gory grime
Questioning look, shell-shocked
A heart plunging in fright and flight

Hands akimbo, life a game of bingo
Puzzles to decode in a winner's game
God a figure, as she stares in a mirror
A figurine too busy to answer her questions.

35.

Summer is so Beautiful

Summer is so beautiful
Not only because the sun is out
To compete and outshine your glow
Failing shamelessly, now it gawps.

Summer is so beautiful
Not only because the grass is green
Not with envy, but to testify
I've outdone the red carpet - at service for a super-celebrity.

Summer is so beautiful
Not only because there is a worthy King
Tending majestically and dutifully
To every need and desire of a Queen.

Summer is so beautiful
Not only because the fruits of your hard-work
Are dropping graciously at your feet
They are also bursting with ripe juicy flavour.

Summer is so beautiful
It has to be, to meet your high standards
In virtuous qualities and selfless service
As you sow seeds of love to many generations.

Why I Write

I write to feed that hunger, make mine a big plate
I write to soothe that ache, bleaching clean the slate
If the body is fed right, and the mind feels alright
Then you and I can tilt our head up to watch the sunrise.

I write to scare away that boredom and loneliness
I write to guard your heart like a nursing lioness
If you're not feeling lonely even when you're alone
Then my poem has done its bit in keeping you company.

I write to speak your mind, when the words you can't find
I write to wipe your tears, caress your fears
The world may bring you gory, let my words remind you of your glory
It's all good news, now smile and be happy.

37.

Sorry

Sorry for the days I turned into nights in vain
Sorry for the nights I lay wide awake and stared
Sorry for the blood I let bleed and clot
And for letting you taste the salty running tears.

Sorry for the non-religious fasting session
Sorry for making you dress in tatters to the palace
Sorry for the abject poverty in midst of plenty
And for making you feel the brunt of my anger.

Sorry for making you count coins to spend
Sorry for making you till and toil on ice.
Sorry for the rosy tomorrow that I'm delaying
And for sowing in the year that locusts abound.

Sorry for the scars I left on your heart
Sorry for the bruises that will never heal
Sorry for the pain I inflicted knowingly
And for those vile thoughts, you were not meant to hear.

Sorry for the dark shadows I never said no to
Sorry for the frogs I shared kisses with
Sorry for the bottle, that failed to mask it all
And for my alter-ego that fails to be happy for me.

38.

Needle's Hole

By their lies, we shall know them
By their truth, we shall recoil in horror
And when the facades have worn thin
In shattered mirror, we shall see their blank stares.

Their walk, almost straight and narrow
Their talk, delectably laced with honey
But they practice not what they preach
And their sermons, more mouth than heart.

The elaborate regalia, a perfect cover
The rehearsed meekness
Indoctrinating tools and ballooning greediness
Far too large to push through the needle's hole.

Religious rites with a dab of spirituality
Resounding Amen and thundering claps
Give unto Caesar, "My name is Caesar";
And getting to God through me, is easier.

My Words

Across many seas and borders
I shall weave a lengthy tightrope
Upon which my words shall sojourn
Bridging the gap of eager minds.

It shall convey messages, pure and undiluted
Of stabbing truth and comforting hues
Collapsing your world into mine
A shared abode that stands the test of time.

Telling you like I'm closer than your shadow
Willing you like the urge of a thousand angels
Soothing away that churning ache and pain
While you float high above the dark clouds.

40.

I Pray

I pray for the victories of David
Revered by men, and loved by God
To go into life's battle unscratched and triumphant
Singing endless praise in Your presence.

I pray for the wisdom of Solomon
Grace to discern between evil and good
A porch full of knowledge and understanding
And a heart to build for You and for men.

I pray for the patience of Abraham
The virtue of waiting for God's time
To know that with You, all is possible, and
Rather than fall prey, to kneel down and pray.

I pray for the faith of Job
Thanking You when the journey is smooth and rosy, and
Trusting You when it's littered with thorns and bumps
Knowing without faith, I can't please You.

I pray for the strength of Samson
Resilient at service for only You
Channelling my energy to help others
And the selflessness of charity.

I pray for the grace of Ruth
Knowing when to plan, and to act
The grace to ask for help when needed
And to maximise all opportunities You've given me.

41

The Only Woman
I Truly Love

Angel I'm not meant to hold
Pure, her heart glows for me
Satisfied, her form flows for me
Precious, her gaze I hold
The only woman I truly love

Loving her, she makes so easy
Unique beauty, like winter sunlight
Graced by virtues, a delightful land
My treasured crown, I'm duty bound
To only woman I truly love

Magical when my smile she returns
Making me skip beats, heart racing
Mystical when my soul she searches
My desires brought to light
By the only woman I truly love

Out of my sight, my heart breaking
Missing her touch, my body aching
Out of my vicinity, my clock clicking
When in my arms, my future beckons
She's the only woman I truly love

A light but I see nothing when with her
A potion my body falling next to her
A wind, all blown away just for her
My diary, my time revolves around her
The only woman I truly love

42.

Its All Over

On the wait,
my eyes glimpse the form
approaching.
Wait no more,
Capture the fleeing minutes
as it's all over.

On the edge
of the horizon
I wait,
pass it on
shadows creeping up on me
for the last assault.

Wrap it up
It's almost over,
Dead silence.
My heart skips
as it all comes crashing down,
Magic melts away.

43.

Fading Sage

Stare at it all day, but you know it not
Too familiar in reckoning with a mirage
Searching fakes all day and night
While binning treasure, too much to manage
You have it all, unused, now losing it
And it's memory erodes with each passing age.

Got diamonds plus a hole in your pocket,
while you store pebbles in your garage;
and at midnight you lose count of
how freely you roam in your cage.
You're upside down and inside out
while taking each breath with a gauge.

So full of it, but now your widows mite,
all dwindled just like your meagre wage;
Into obscurity what used to be your might,
such a shame, you're now a fading sage.
Let's hope posterity, in colours paint
your story when we turn the page.

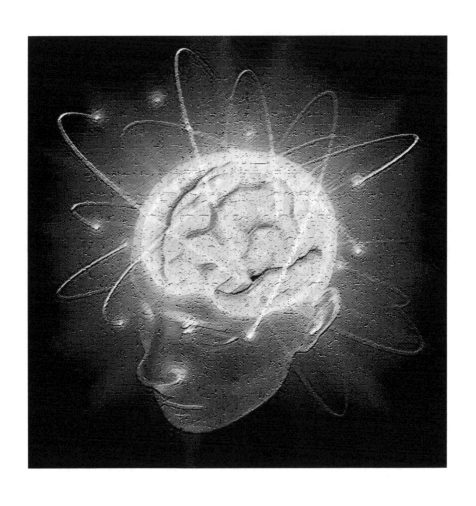

44.

Human Mind

In shrouded clouds your thoughts bellow,
Deep and complex, going an inch deeper.
You're like me, a stranger fellow,
Who piles bile and stores blood till it gets darker

It smokes out, seeping through the gallows;
You mask it in shades, a trained liar,
Who watches when wind blows it low,
For characters and acts come near and far.

It astounds and confounds lest any sorrow;
Gets you lost till you stand aloft on Mars.
Maybe you'll fathom it by tomorrow,
Until then heavy laden your mind bears.

We are soldiers of conscience in row,
Who shed skins, not scenes like a sleeper;
And grasp till we gasps for more to borrow,
Into a mind where it rarely matters.

45.

Fair Trade

Trading with you, so much fun
Grading it's price, so much pun
Stating the profit, a perfect con
Daylight robbery called fair trade

What sort of trade happens in reverse?
Buyers determine the price to buy
Farmers victims of their hard-work
Sellers, coerced to the only option given.

My sweat dried up by the scorching sun
My flat pocket a harsh reality of deceit
My children wallow in hunger and misery
But feeding other children of the world is fair.

Fair trade, to you fair
To me, just another nightmare
Reminds me of my fathers' days
In those sugarcane plantations

When demand equals supply
Both parties parting with a smile
My children, a better future secured
Then that's when trade is fair.

46.

7 Billion People

So many people but it's just me
So many people but it's just you
I look at them and see no face
All but a blurred vision
For I am to them, another person
Scrounging and scraping
Scarcity in the midst of abundance
My body aching in protest
My stomach in the contest
But I am just one of 7 billion people

So many people but it's just me
So many people but it's just you
I open my mouth but no words came out
My mind is gagged like my mouth
All I am is another threat
Shouting and screaming
At increasing injustice and war
My ear echoing their deeds
My world is corrupted by their seeds
But I am just one of 7 billion people.

So many people but it's just me
So many people but it's just you
I take a sniff and churn up
And my vomit is like the next
Rotten like society
Leaders all out in war for their own pockets
Enlarging the dichotomy between poor and rich
All I want is freedom and fair play
But all I smell is bondage and foul play
But I am just one of 7 billion people.

47.

Whisper a Noise

An earache amidst serenity
Driving me wild enough to reconsider
Earplugs or getting accustomed
To unending monotonous routine.

To listen, I need to lip-read
Sight limited to split seconds
Drive restricted by inner urge
Such a voice, a whisper of noise

A queen bee in an anthill
No uphill task can turn it home
And my companion the only solace
In this downhill to obscurity.

A whisper so deafening
Vibrating in my ear
The empty vase makes the loudest noise
Leaving my mind echoing.

48.

Journey

All come and go on this journey
Not a path for the faint hearted
And from all walks of life they come
To arrive at that desired destination

Not in pace or step they walk
Going that distance only mind can see
And in this journey of life
It's not how far but how well

Some with baggage come
Dragging lives with them
While some travel light
Run or stroll, it matters not

There is no medal for being first
No shadow cast for being last
But multiplies what you add
All die cast, all staked in.

49

She Likes to Play

Seems like I have it written boldly
Across my head, no words minced
A fool with skull so thick
Her scrubbing mat to dumb her dirt

She wants me as a backup plan
A fool's paradise in her palm
To be deactivated on her whim
When something better comes along

She wants to get involved alright
A temporary measure to pass the time
Just not good enough to be permanent
In a little twisted scheme of life

"Life isn't always fair", she says
But hers, as perfect as can be
Be another pawn in her game
All sacrificed for her tiny happiness

Today's pain for tomorrow's happiness
Logs thrown in to keep it burning
Body warmed and the logs turn ashes
A friend indeed thinks of others happiness

50.

Deal or No Deal

Western world
Come dine and party with me
Dip and dive into your corruption
I'm just your enemy's friend
I gain nought being your enemy
Making shady deals in the shade
Shaking hands and not heads
What I want, I'll get anyway
Either play ball or play bombs
Either way, I always win
I have done it before, I will do it again
No longer called colonisation, it's commonwealth
Don't call it slavery, call it sojourn
Back then, shiny metal for your children.
And once dumb, always so
Now, here is the better deal!
My Swiss accounts for your soul
My foreign aid for your future
Deal or no deal?

African Leaders
Seems like a good deal to me
I will dine with you and more
As long as you scratch my back
I will scratch yours
While I drag back my loot
Round belly and fat pockets
Ignore my scaly of a people
If all collapses, promise me this
A narrow passage from it all
Foreign currency to weaken us

Blow our mind and economy
When my wealth is worthless
Set up agents to spit on us
Destroying our land and livelihood
While siphoning our treasures
A tight leash called immigration
Seeping out the best of our seeds
Though your land maybe snow-filled
We call it our own greener pastures
An Oxbridge or Harvard education
To hypnotise us that ours is inferior
I'm sure, we will never know
As your grand design only dazzles us,
At your bigger picture, we are blown

51.

Opposite Ends

Stuck in the atmosphere of my breath
Hanging for dear life by those puffs
So laboured it's weight shakes my shell
My heart the victim of my decision
Says flee, but my limbs are fright-filled
And panic disarms before battle starts

Lights shuts off as my eyes succumb
Heart heavy by its daily burden
I daren't hope as it might come true
Better still swap my life for another
All passes by and I feel so old
Past stands by, I'm shutting down

Those dreams, complete irony
Of foul play by my sub-consciousness
Fatal turn, all let loose
To go back, many hearts lost
Sooner some doors will be open
And the bird will surely fly away

Of my sleep, I want to wake up
From bed full of nails
Maybe the nightmares might subside
and a genuine smile return to my face.
Happiness and love ought to be found in same pod
but often, at opposite ends they stand

52.

Yawn

Not on my face.
The gush of air;
Stale
As you fight sleep.

Like a disease
Spreads like wild fire.
Don't pass the bug,
It's contagious.

Involuntary
Nerves twitching
It's very late,
I'm yawning now.

The more you fight,
The more you yawn.
Hands can't stifle
The release of air.

Writing this poem,
Caused me to yawn.
Reading the poem,
Will make you yawn.

53.

Twisted Truth

How can lies becomes truth,
And the deed end before it starts?
The twist of events to change history
Or web of lies woven to alter the future.
Whatever the case, it isn't right.
As your words apparently weigh more
And the fact, a glimpse into reality.

How can the right thing be wrong
And whip cracked to say thanks?
The downfall though envisaged
Yet it's build up to materialise
All in the height of wickedness
Where evil suppresses the just.
And justice, a long endless journey.

Your limbs quiver as you say it
Your feet on heat aftermath
The tell-tale signs for all to see
Only we see just what we want
And the truth, your interpretation
No concerns whose horse is garrotted
As long as the truth stays a lie.

54.

Being Alive

You think I don't deserve to smile?
Or scream out in sheer ecstasy
and pretend all is well, till it is;
Just because you think you had it worse.

You said I don't soak my bed in tears,
Cuddling my pillow till the fluff comes out
or toss in bed till day breaks,
but guess what, I have lost count!

Losing grasp of the order in the day,
All collapsing and crashing down
Fear as the wall closes in,
This and much more, my close companion.

An account soaked deep in blood,
Backward glance for the loan shark trail,
More mail and the heart sinks,
Mine sinks way past revival.

The salty tears and familiar ache,
The will to stay back on the floor,
Head banging till all cracks open,
Yet here I am still standing.

I can smile 'cause I still breathe,
I can also weep 'cause I'm alive,
Live a fantasy or lost in daydreams;
The power of staying alive.

Attaining immortality -
Zeros the power to make a choice,
Only the free will to accept all,
Optimising opportunities on the way.

55.

Figure Eight

She is one of a kind
Her two eyes I barely see
Staring at her like a 3D screen
For her, I would gladly go on all fours
Kissing her five beautiful fingers
Like six proud preened peacocks
My stop is the seventh one
But her figure eight's got me transfixed
Now the train has passed the ninth
But in my book, she is ten out of ten.

Forget Me Not

Please don't turn in this direction
As you might see me cowering
Shaking and shivering with
The terror of being found out.

I don't like hiding like a criminal
A saint I am, bare minimal
My acts cleaned up, not an animal
Few slips up counted in decimal

Your eyes see all, Omnipresence
Conceive my deeds before my senses
I can't hide them, all revealed, my
Guilty pleasures and addictions.

I need Your help and maybe Your lashes
Forgive me but don't forget me
Turning a new page, a new me
Fighting temptation of looking back.

A Piece of Me

Fake a smile, tears roll out
Shake a hand, dagger drawn out
Take a bite, all puked out
All the time, all the way

Say a word, queries pile up
Shed a pound, trouble streams up
Phone a friend, all gang up
Feed the mind, take the soul

Have a laugh, it's all on me
Pack the load, it's all for me
Place the blame, on top of me
Say your piece, a piece of me

58.

Tick and Tuck

Tick and tuck
Goes that hand of clock
Tick and tuck
Repeating
My weary gaze keeps company
With the hands of the clock

Tick and tuck
Is all I can hear
Tick and tuck
No other sound
In this eerie space of mine
My heart beats to it.

Tick and tuck
It's not tuck and tick
Tick and tuck
It stays the same
Why not two ticks or two tucks?
My heart beats the same way.

59.

Quarter to Nine

Every step towards the dream
Stretch myself to the aim
No opponent can try to maim
My willpower to the fame
'Cos all obstruction will become
Crumbled dirt in the clay
My motto never to blame
Other players in the game
I slip and fall in the shame
Like a knight with no dame
So many needs yet no dime
Tempted to a life of crime
The devil invites me to dine
Life fast forward to my demise
All these thoughts I must deny
Purge my heart of all the grime
I see myself in my prime
Gather the world on my palm
My soul mate in my realm
My heart and soul now in a beam

Say goodbye to when I was deranged
I know I'm quarter to the time
A life of bliss, here I come
quarter to nine, but not yet dim
To possess and then lay claim
Years that have gone to waste
Wandering aimlessly with no plan.

60.

Cursed Love

I can't do this anymore
A fly buzzing me to grave,
My favourite curse.

Can't stand her presence,
Destined to nag me to death,
But miss her in her absence.

I'm spent loving her,
She takes but gives no love,
I've fallen for her.

My life is so messed up,
I'm tangled in web of lies
of her love for me.

My soul-mate she claims,
Yet she cares not but for herself,
And leaves my heart in shreds.

61.

One-Man Army

It hurt so much, I'm past caring
and it's no use me crying,
as they gang up to see me failing,
they may be right as I'm done trying,
to see it all happening.

My blood wishes me success or not,
Dead set at making me go nuts.
My mind corrupted, going to rot,
Messed up like I'm a smoking pot,
And everything is my own fault.

So much pain, and it spills over;
So many shots, as I take cover;
My heart is so crushed, by this tsunami;
In this war, I'm a one-man army
and defeat is imminent.

62.

Tunnel of Life

Life is a tunnel,
dark enough to make you fall,
full of barriers and struggle,
each day, a test of will.

A few more steps and sweat,
a little determination,
a mind that never says NO,
when deep in the dark.

Lift your head up high,
all tunnels come to an end,
and the reward is the light
that dries off all tears.

The pain is worth it,
though the barriers are daunting,
no help in sight but within
as you never give up.

63.

Betrayed Eagle

My heart like a balloon you pierce
With fury of a baboon so fierce
In crushing ache I double in tears
As my blood gush and ooze out my fears

Trust shattered like grains of blown rice
Friends scattered for their share of dire price
My body bloodied by your arrows and stained gears
I'm bared open, a hunted game for wild bears

You got your sieve out to collect my dry cries
Beneath your sleeves, a dagger to pluck out my eyes
You so close to me, in more ways than one
Yet you stab me deep, am fading off and worn.

You've done your worst, you gave it your all
Over the cliff, you push and expects me to fall
Look again before you blow out your horn
An eagle soaring high, watching you shrink and gone.

64

Girl of the World

She is my girl of the world
who plays dress-up all day,
and seeks my attention with
her whims, moans, and drama.
In the house she is always there,
in front of the mirror making up.
She's white in the morning and
she turns orange in the evening,
'cause that's the way of the world,
and to mix, she must blend.

Outside the house, she is everywhere;
grasping for attention,
in front of the lads,
and eyeing up any paparazzi
who ask her for a close-up
while I'm left mopping up after her.
Her upbringing is not to blame,
society tells her how to wear her hair;
how she must garnish it,
like a celebrity with flowers.
They tell her in the magazines;
how wearing less is more
and how she must pout her lips
which must be dripping, blood-red
to be that girl of the world.

They lecture her through the media -
bizarre antics rather than good morals.
The price to pay for fame
must not be up for bargaining;
she must be ready to do anything
as long as she is in front of the lens,
and be that girl of the world.

What I want matters not,
I daren't tell her I want that girl
who wakes up looking like an angel,
whose virtues I fall in love with,
and who unlike the girl of the world;
is the girl that makes my world.

65.

Celestial Girl

I can stare at you all day and night
Like the stars in the sky at night
You dazzle me when you twinkle
And tonight, I'm lost in your sparkle.

Just like the moon beams at night
Like a diamond, you reflect the light
And in my life, you ignite the flame
That glows and warms my soul.

You're the sun that clears my clouds
A perfect touch to dry my tears
And when thunders strike its chords
You're always there to clear my fears.

66

A Fool

I'm made a fool
Or I made myself one
'Cos I am not pushed into it
Nudged but not pushed
And like a fool I feel.

I look like a fool
It is not about what I wear
A bit about what I did
And with years of regret
I think like a fool.

My mind screams I'm one
For knowing what to do
And like a fool I'm scared
To roll the wheel of the unknown
And make right the wrong.

I'm happy being a fool
But I'm getting used to it
And I query even logic
To justify understanding
How foolish I can be.

67.

My Useless Man

Where is that useless man of mine?
At twelve midnight he's not back home,
and neither was he yesterday nor the day before.
He clocks in at 10am at work daily,
his mates clock out by 5pm,
an hour's drive should do the magic
to settle with me for the night.

Where is that useless man of mine?
Not that I suspect him of anything,
so faithful like an obese dog,
not bothered by all the talk
of him visiting some cheap whore.
A lipstick stain, a woman's number
doesn't mean he is a cheat.

Where is that useless man of mine?
Some says he prowls the street;
a spectacle for all to behold,
reeking of fumes and vomit.
Not the type to complain about
his swaying walk or slurry words,
I sober not when I'm alone.

Where is that useless man of mine?
I hope he won't be the death of me!
His wages not for food or family;
at the Bookies he downs the lot,
An addict, so don't blame him.
Good thing that I work,
to pay off some of his debt.

Where is that useless man of mine?
Although he's not here, when he is home
all my needs he satisfies,
and like a queen he make me feel.
When he's out, I feel useless,
no one to blame or bitch at;
that's why he is not that useless.

68.

In Utmost Reverence

In utmost reverence we bow our heads
Desiring His presence to fill our hearts
We crave none, all glory ascribe to You
Hoping our dense yet empty lives be blessed.

Our senses You own, no interest
In utmost reverence we bow our heads
As You mould our lives and wills in Your great plan
Hence we question not Your reasons.

The might of Your power we fathom not
The depth of Your love, each day we owe
You anchor our destiny, no plan can change
Surrendering all, nought to hold back
In utmost reverence we bow our heads.

69.

Yetunde

Yetunde, mother has come again
With a big bang she arrives
Not that I ought to be nervous
About why she came.

Yetunde, mother has come again
Such a beauty, all men's poison
She stares at me, I see a star
And like a fool, I'm hypnotised.

Yetunde, mother has come again
No unfinished business to attend
One lifetime just isn't enough
To etch her dreams in our mind.

Yetunde, mother has come again
Dazzling me, I'm in a trance
Puzzling me, a knot best left alone
A rare jewel, all finders keepers.

70.

She Wants me Now

She wants me now
Now that I have sold my soul
Someone else's meat to chew
All emotions drained
The last sweat spent
And words turn to gibberish.
Many years down the drain
And all for love,
Although it seems more like for hate
Act like a fool one more time
And love her totally.

She wants me now;
Now that memories I barely know
All that is left are my regrets
Reminds me just why not to be
When to my pleas, a deaf ear she turns
And my tears she calls fake
All words to no avail
As her heart she locks away
To a better man the key she gives
While I'm left to start over.

She wants me now
After she left me in the lurch
As her standard I can't reach
And her game I can't beat
All my fault when it goes wrong
And she is perfect in all ways
A villain in her fictional tales
Now she blinks twice, I'm all she sees
Though my wound is healed, I've still got the scar
Why I would never be with you?

71.

Point of No Return

She throws a fuss, he catches it
Emotions raw and flaring wild
Competing with words battering
More than enough has been said
Nudging each other to that point
Point of no return.

No need to strike a blow, one already got hurt
Words are mightier than swords
Who throws the first matters no more
Lots of water under the bridge
And standing aloft at opposite ends
Yearning to close up to one point.

Memories that would rather be forgotten
More regrets come into play
That shouldn't have been allowed
Why beat a dead horse anyway?
Like a business they'd rather cut their losses
Walking towards the point of no return.

The divorce isn't usually messy
Bar greediness and sentiment
The professionals set it off
Divide and rule, hopefully amicably
Definitely passed that dreaded point
Point of no return.

72.

Am I Bothered?

Bleed, let it drop, the floor won't mind,
Cry and whimper, let it ring out
I'm used to it, I don't know the difference;
The laughing or the wailing
Letting all go, it will be for nothing
Go cold, iced, and you will still be alone
The world is too busy to notice.

I care, trust me, I really do
But I'm too busy to notice myself
It's not like you aren't on my list
But you are way off the first
You're hurting, but I'm grieving for
My lost soul, my lost values
Misplaced priorities in a corrupt world.

I might be looking at you
But I'm actually staring into space
Head tilted makes me not a good listener
I don't even know you're talking
My nonchalant ways aren't inborn
I'm just moulded by societal norms
Don't call me selfish, it's just survival

You criticise me like that's going to work
You counsel me, but you need it too
My needs comes first in my world
In yours, I expect nothing less
Make a fuss, be a drama queen
All to my overdue entertainment
As I won't still blink.

73.

Blame Game

She stares, she forgets herself
He winks, then more, tears running
Blame her mum, ridiculously gorgeous
Blame his dad, irresistible handsome
But thank yourself you're not the one
Your plain face isn't at fault, it's me.

So elegant, glowing like the only star in sky
So suave, so buff, he's worth nicking
Blame her inner beauty, so dominant
Blame societal values, never him
For your low self-esteem, blame yourself
Then everyone else, but never me.

Her wit defies age and logic
His intellect greater than he can exhaust
Blame her genes, not her jeans
His upbringing is clearly at fault
But not your distracted and empty mind
That can't simply keep up.

I blame you before you blame me
Because someone definitely is at fault
I can accept responsibility and own up
But where's the fun be in that?
It goes pear-shaped and you take the flak
Never my fault in the blame game.

74.

Ashes of a Giant

Ashes on my head, I walk in a daze
Like an outcast ghost, I count no days
Out of luck, I made no case
Blaming it on ill-luck, or just fate
Life is drama, full of tragic scenes
Drowning in it, no one to save
You yearn and will, nothing to show
I dream to live, not in a cage
I crave for the life I see on the page
So heavenly, I want to die
Because every day I rage
Of how much is never enough
Confused -whether to love or to hate
Many fangs too many to count
All waiting to suck and bleed me dry
Blood ties tying me in bondage
My child cries not, nor does my wife
Family expectations and made promises
And every day I bear the shame
Commissions and bills I paid in late
Debt up to my neck, face I must save
Out of my wits, I can hardly breathe
My heart skips a beat when the phone goes
Shadows on my trail, running a mile
Faces I meet, never a smile
Stories to tell, some worse than mine
Every day, just like yesterday
Hoping for when all this will end
So much hate, I can hardly breathe
Haunted daily like game in the wild
Howling loud as I see myself slide

In a crowd, yet no one by my side
Friends hang me up to fry
My tears keep me company
I tasted, it's better than salt
Like a plague, it's bound to spread
For everyday, it's but a routine
Even in my hole, a stand to take
Resigned to fate or break the yoke
Ashes on my head, it must be purged
Ashes on my way, it must be laid rest
Ashes in my world, I know you not.

75.

Waterloo

To most, Waterloo means doomed
To me, it's where I struck gold
Not only because it paves the way to you
Or creates an ideal no man's land
But it's where I first felt you feel me
Get warmed by the heat oozing
From your body to equal mine
Uneasy and tempting fate to start
But in a daring gesture I ventured
Into the soulful yet overwhelming moment
Followed by the unique embrace
Like no other, familiarly embracing
That explained it all to me
Even before I felt your soft lips
Trembling with sheer passion
And the desire that took over
Though short yet memorable
So much to do but no time
I felt your reluctance as it ended
As eyes spoke volumes
Of how you wanted to capture and freeze
The moment and make it evergreen
Could we be sure to work this out?

I see you and I dream away
Into a future where nothing matters but us
You see me and you crave
For the advantages while it lasts
The promise of this and so much more
I want to share all with you
My blood, sweat and tears
My name, pain and gain
Building together and sharing
Our life in an adorable castle
With a garden filled with pets
Gushing in sheer admiration
Our sight set as we care and tend
Our children in the union
Of our love and togetherness

It's Not You, it is Me

Her love she strung so high
Like a kite with no thread
An angel I must be to collect
And when I do, must let go

Her game, she sets the rules
Play along and you just might
Play her card, so close to the heart
All set to lose, except her

Two steps forward, it all seems
All dreams set to come true
In a blink, she rolls the dice
Three steps backwards, it's her call

Why play a game you can't win?
She dances to all but your tune
Minces not her words when she says
It's not you, it is me.

Her type of Love

My heart in her hand, I choke
My time at her will, I release
My way in her way, I freeze
A prey in the game, she hunts.

My body like a tool, she plies
My goal and her aim, are one
My dance to her music, her delight
My pain is her gain, a game.

I run while she walks, we arrive
I work while she waits, to reap
She jokes and I smile, because I'm the joke
She sleeps, I dream her nightmares.

I cook, she eats, I choke
Her present, her past, my future
I hope she believes my destiny
My hand she leads, to my fall.

She forgives, I forget I'm now haunted
I forget, she remembers my wrongs
I see, and she sees through me
I walk for her, she walks all over me.

She's broke, I'm broken to her demand
A god, my worship never ceases
My debt for her love, must be paid
For life, her type of love, I must love.

78.

She's My Second Chance

How can I love her this much
When myself I hate as much?
Hers a will to live and dream
Mine a wish to drop all and let go.

How can she mean so much to me
When to myself I barely count?
She is so valuable yet she knows it not
My life is worth as much as a grain of salt.

She sees in life all she ever wants
I walk through it all with futile effort
She imagines, she wills, she just believes
My faith and hope, just a mirage.

Through it all she travels light
By the yoke of my baggage, I'm bent
For her love, my slate I clean
To see my second chance, I change.

How I can start again, she explains
When her voice rings out, all storms calm
For her smile, all set to roll
In my life, my second chance.

Her Web of Desire

Her hair is like she is: all gold
Her eyes, so clear, all blue
She walks like she conquers all
And talks like whispers of the wind
Her smiles all come without hesitation
She thinks once, we think twice
Her body like a figurine
Like a conspiracy of the gods
Tempting your entire will
You can't ignore it, but can't be caught
Not helped by her choice of chains
All there you can't but miss
Like a poison yet you want a taste
Contagious like a virus
All set to wreak havoc in your brain.
But we all know she's got a phobia
She hears it and she is shrieking
That sounds almost like glass shattering
But I can't be caught writing this
It will seem like I'm captured
In her web, a spider's dinner
As she spins it, her desire.

80.

Who is She?

Like a ghost she cruises
In a daze she wakes
For a future she ventures
Today's debt to deal with
Her independence she depends on
Her family she rallies
Her job her gateway
Her innocence she fakes
Her love she hates
Her identity she defines
So vague and amorphous
Her eyes searching your soul
Her lips tell you nothing
But you crave a kiss
Her body almost ageless
Her mind queries logic
Her health she watches
Like an eagle, many games no deal
Her skin so magnetic
Electrifying on contact
She wishes, yet so in tune
To station herself to reality.

Who is she?
In abstract she defines herself
I dare define her
In volumes her stoic stare
Like the wrath of a scorned woman
She wreaks havoc,
And hungers to take a bite.
So diverse her sprung surprises
Yet so angelic her simple nature
Like a sin of the gods
Her confounded mind confuses
I ask who she is
The answer she knows not.

81.

Love Letter

It ought to start with how much
I have fallen for her
But reasoning dictates otherwise.
Rather it brought to reckoning
The aches and pains she caused
Watching the one I love
Love someone else more
Blame love, never her.

Second place I occupy
Gladly lapping leftover affection.
I dream, she dreams too
Mine of her, hers of her lover
Straining to impress her
Only telling her of what ought to be
A loser so full of insecurity
Holding a pitiful stance

Blame love, never me
In a fantasy my heart dwells
She loves me not
Dependable hands, a stranger's face
The realistic option her world dictates
Justifying myself as her plaything
But heavy my heart as I pen
To her my love letter.

82.

Can't Wait

Can't wait to see your face
To hold you in my arms
To hug you so close I can't breathe
To get lost in your soulful eyes
To feel your skin next to mine
To dream so much with you
To whisper words in your ears
And connect our thoughts
Even when I stop waiting.

Can't wait to feel you
And make you shudder
To make you moan my name
Like the only thing that matters
To synchronise with my rhythm
As we dance together
To hear your voice as you join me
And we have to wait no more.

Can't wait to make you mine
Changing your name as we unite
Waking up to you every morning
Gazing at beauty that has no equals
Praying that I see you againthe next day
For all my life I wish nothing else
A virtuous lady, no blemish
In my sight, so flawless
Anything good is worth the wait
But for your love, I can't wait.

83.

In Real Life

Woke up and set out to find
The reason I slept less last night
Having you occupy my mind -
Not a bad reason to lose sleep
For I went to sleep thinking of you
Hoping to meet you in my dreams
As you willed me to free myself
And do more than I could imagine
In real life.

Last night you captured my sleep
The more I tried, the more Iwas awakened
By everything that reminded me of you
Reliving our first date and kiss
Daydreaming about our first baby
And planning how to return
The favour and make you love me too
How I willed my fantasy
To be real.

Last night how I yearned
To hold you close to me and stand in
The winter cold and summer blues
Tracing waves on your glittering skin
Getting lost in your soulful eyes
Nodding off to your soft voice
And wishing you could only hear
How my heart beat for every event
In every situation of your life.

Last night I let myself go
Into the distance and wandered…
How my heart aches and
My veins pump for your touch
My body longing for your warmth
My breath calling out your name
Dreams are empty when you are absent
And my soul screams out for you
To be my all in real life.

84.

What am I Feeling?

A good friend with more to give
With such a smile you can't resist
Tempting all my will to yield
Before I know it's crept on me
My mind thinks of what to be
Body aches to feel your touch
Your lips on me, dreams come true
In your embrace my heart will melt
Every time wishing forever it would last
And you ask what am I feeling

In a golden vase I gladly gave
My whole heart feverishly to love
Giving every inch of me
In your world my mansion stood
With you in my sight my vision is clear
Gazing on you, my future glows
By your side, I want to grow
In your touch, I feel fulfilled
In distress doubled with desire
I ask myself what am I feeling

By your lips I melt so fast
Savouring the moment with awe
Cake and chocolate can't compete
The sweet taste budding in me
Your words like an ocean wave
Spectacular and beautiful yet strong
Keeping vigil thinking of you
Day dreaming of dancing with you
Our bodies gliding like one

Melodies in our heart we sing
Making it last in ecstasy
As we ask what are we feeling

Your presence ignites a change
All the rules you make me break
Bluffing consequences in an instant
Impulse you make me love
Your babies I want to hold
Your tears I want to dry
Your laughter I want to cradle
In your dreams, I want to live
Feeling you and filling you
Is what I am feeling.

85.

My Son My Soul

Doting and loving
My heart filled with warmth
My eyes and hands must steady
The new friend I created

His tiny fingers clasp mine
His intense eyes searches me
With racing heartbeat I pray
That my love for him falters not

So angelic, such innocence melts my soul
He gives me his trust
Carefree in his ways as he hopes
That I protect him always.

I can't but love him
His contagious smile he shares
His rosy cheek glow
Making happiness abound

Soul-mate we're ordained to be
Connected by The Supernatural
In hearts, hands and minds
To make oneness of our destinies.

86.

The Chase

She likes me, she likes me not
Beaming smiles, alluring stare
So confusing you somersault
Flirting like she hates you
Hating that she flirts with you
And so the chase begins.

She wants nothing to do with you
'Cause you might just ticks all the boxes
Yet she reckons something is amiss
Finding it she wills herself not
Twice bitten never shy from
Escaping the chaser's grasp.

Taking the challenge you're resolute
Just a little bit more, you love her
Daring all you become determined
Her love you must have
Like a race with one crown
And the winner takes all: her heart.

A mind-reader, no gimmicks will work
A soul-searcher, no hidden places
Like a hypnotist loving her job
Her heart conditioned, never wavering
Racing with all your might, you find she's always ahead
And the player is being played.

Finally, everything is made clear
Loving is a gift, it must be freely willing
The heart is too powerful to be caged
By wit, cajoling, gimmicks and lies
It chooses whoever it desires
That no amount of chasing can undo.

87.

Brown Coat and Green Scarf

In brown and green she likes them all
In gazette style, she lets it roll
To work, to play and to the mall
Her identity she makes prior
In military style she fights her war
So determined she stands it all
No curse or vanquish can defeat
Her brown coat and green scarf.

Round her neck she gently wraps
Tight to her body she firmly clasps
On her pad she diligently taps
All her way around the maps
In her diary she fills the gaps
Effortlessly she sways her hips
Two heavy bags her daily trips
In brown coat and green scarf.

In her eyes you can't miss
The loving gaze that is released
Fears and emotions that confuse
Your mind as her form teases
Time stands still and the moment freezes
Her magic touch your doubts disprove
Making you want to remove
Her brown coat and green scarf.

88.

She's More than that

A lady with so many pages to turn
Voluminous, makes many heads turn
So alluring, makes many men to burn
She chews and spits them out in turn
Don't read her, lest you get fatigued and fall
But to the few that she owes and loves
To them she commits her all in blood
No half measures, it's all in or all out.

She spins them dizzy with her mood
'Cos she is that crazy;
Gets them salivating for her food,
She's tasty, but she's not that easy.
She loves to nudge and push till they jump
And if her wit fails, she grabs them brazenly
And not always to make them squeak
To the lucky ones, it is more than that.

She spurs, strokes and fill their cups;
They're intoxicated and run over.
She twirls, sways and rocks herself,
Till they back away and take cover.
She coos, hums and leads them on
No holds barred, just a step further.
Her claws she dips, her grip she tightens
Their brains she tips, and their souls she frightens
But they're bound in chains as her lovers.

89.

Where are You?

It's no use crying
But she does
Anyway
It's no use talking
But she talks
Continuously
First to herself, and then
To the curtain in her hand
While she gazes long and hard
Down the dark, lonely road
Then she gives it a gentle stroke, a caress
And in a little whisper asks
"Where are you?"

This is not the first time
More than once before, she's stood
Colours coming off the curtain now,
And the road, a constant reminder
Of the culprit and the victim
And herself, a distant audience.
And the show continues
While she asks same inane question
Meant for none but herself
"Where are you?"

For the umpteenth time, the same question
"Where are you?"
She needs that warmth,
That comfort - her reality.
But here she stands, all by herself
Transparent, it's like a curse
The gods are doing a stand up
She is the joke with make up
But here she is clutching a chipped cup
Not for a toast, but for same question
Where are you?

Bottles run out now
A drunk fool, needs a seat
Or precisely what she is, an easy lay
Except this time the bed stays silent
No more squeaking, just her alone
It's three days late, then she feels it
A twinge, then she sees it
The familiar red hue, is all she needs
A massive relief, no more jokes.
While she drapes herself
In that warmth, that comfort
And in her reality.

90.

Midnight Daydreams

Awake but tense I lay
In my bed where it all awaits
Not at the door nor a blot to bade
But in my head, and so I wake.

Pitch dark, no cocks to crow
Singular laid, no snores to share,
No shadows or echoes to interject
Yet wide awake with starry eyes.

To sleep, I search my head
For ghost to lay to rest
But soul too wandering to care,
To act and learn the lines.

In my sleep I am but dreaming
A rosy one, not a nightmare
But now I'm daydreaming
Being an Emir, not a silly mare.

91.

Saw Akudaya in London

Met her on my way to work
On a bright day with blue sky
In a corner she sat on the train
Dressed for the part
For a day in court or for a funeral
"Shola!" I screamed and lightened up
For a second, I thought I will be blanked
But then she creases into a smile
An all-knowing and familiar one
Showing her gap-toothed signature
Wow, what a reunion!

It's been five or six years now
How times flies
And what a chance meeting you again
Across many seas
Stories to share, gaps to fill
With my long lost childhood friend.
But this is not to be as her stop is next
And mine - miles away.
But let's swap contact numbers
Can't wait to call home and let them know I saw you! I exude
Her colour fades, it must be the wintery air
As she alights at London Bridge station.
And disappears into the crowd

Hello Tunji, you won't believe who I've just seen.
It's only your childhood crush!
How we used to tease you both back then.
Really Addie- and who might that be?
It's Shola.
Which Shola?
Your Shola, Sholese!
Hello! Hello!! Poor network again…
Mate, I'm here, nothing wrong with the network
Oh! Why the silence then Tunji?
Addie, it's because there's something wrong with your brain.
Joking and trivialising my pain and sadness
Of all people, I don't expect this callousness from you.
What !! What have I done now Tunji?
Rubbing salt in an open wound Addie
And reawakening these painful emotions.
Tunji, I don't understand what you're saying.
Addie, I was there when they buried Shola two days ago!!
What? What did you just say Tunji?
Shola died a week ago in a car crash Addie!
But Tunji… er… em I……….

Hours after speaking with Tunji,
Double-checking with other friends,
Reading tons of "rest in peace" messages
On various social media profiles
I'm left shell-shocked and shivering
Heart racing fast, and limbs quavering,
Palms sweaty and brain whizzing
Nothing to do with her tragic demise
Or how I missed the dreadful news

What my body is asking my brain is -
Who did I see this morning?
Either my eyes were deceiving me
Or my brain is playing a cruel joke on me
I can't be having a mental breakdown, or can I?
I search for my phone frantically
The exchanged contact details will suffice,
And sure enough Shola's name stares back at me
I'm definitely sane and I know what I saw
Didn't only see her,
We also hugged, talked, joked, laughed, and waved
With a promise to call her on her phone.
I know what any sane person would do
No, not that - definitely not calling the number.
Its best I delete the number and
Pretend I saw no one this morning
Best way to resolve this dilemma
Albeit the coward's route
My personal motto - better safe than sorry.
And just as I'm about to press delete button
Fate deals a sudden hand and
My worst nightmare comes calling -
As my phone belts out
Fela's "Suffering n Smiling" tune
Indicating an incoming call.
Oh my God - it's Shola calling
I'm getting a phone call from Akudaya

To pick or not to pick the call
Covered instantly in anxious sweat
Don't suppose I've got time to have a panic attack

In a trance
I hit the answer button, hold my breath,
And wait to drop dead.
A sickening twist
"Hello."
I'm in such a state
I almost fail to notice it's another voice
"Saw your number on my partner's phone".
A few seconds to compose myself
Then I say "Partner?? Er… who are you?"
"I'm Francis - but who are you?" the voice replies
Who am I in this situation? - preferably a nobody.
But my response shocks even me
"Who is your partner if you don't mind me asking?"
"Shola. But you are yet to answer me?"
"I'm er…em, my name is er…."
And just as I'm about to say my name
I hear the voice in the background
Distinctive and familiar
So surreal it sent shocking waves through me
It's Shola's voice asking -
"Who's is that Darling?"
Not sure why
I did what I did next -
I hung up.

Akudaya is the name Yoruba people used in their mythology story for dead people who are seen living elsewhere far away, from people who are aware of their being dead.

92.

Wasted Love

A wise man says,
"we serves all and everyone
but ourselves".
In the quest
we burn our candles
at both ends like the elves.
And our reward for this are
Scars, tears and smoked lens.
As we are hell-bent on
hanging memory on the wall,
trophies on the shelves,
and ourselves on the tree.
All in our quest for justifying
why blood is thicker,
friendship forever,
and you and I together.

It's like a deal between
Valley and the sea
One is got lot of love to give
The other, nothing to lose
And the more I give and share
The more you take and cheer
The more I slave and save
The more you whip and waste.
And like a sinking hole that are
I watch you take all in whole
Not that you don't have a soul,
It's because you don't have a goal.

Logic dictates maybe I should me the wise man
Who loves none but himself
Shower myself with love and cares
But if that means missing your caress
Then I rather be a fool in love
Where my all in love is wasted on you
My blood and sweat is smeared on you
And maybe you might justify in future
Why blood is thicker
Friendship forever
And you and I together.

Peaceful Chaos

We live in a box where all is pile up
Boxes, baggage and clothes all over
Human piled and tripping each other
And our breath we share in one cup

It's a long queue to use the toilet
We cooked meals with our skin roasted
Our snores and wakes we rehearse on one bed
As we're covered in clothes like that for ballet

Our tears and sweats we use as bath waters
And for breakfast, we regurgitate our dinner
And when you scream, we thought why whisper?
As we sit perilously on the edge of our counters

Our windows and doors, one and the same
They serve same purpose, entry and exit
For strangers near and families that don't exist
And these peaceful chaos, drives us insane

My Future Ambition

There he stands shaking
Like a leaf in winter
Before the stony-faced and indifferent
Stare of the stern questionnaire
Until he is hit with it -
What is your future ambition?

He scratches his head
Looks forwards, backwards
And up at the still white ceiling
That refuses to come to the aid
Of his future ambition.

He remembers his brother
Years after his graduation
Still roaming the streets in worn-soled shoes
Looking for all the filled vacancies
As his skeletal frame keeps thinking
Of his future ambition.

How will he be certain of the answer
When the present is doubtful?
How secure is the future
When the security of the present is at stake?
Yet he expects an answer
To what he will be in future.

In despair and frustration
He voices out with all his might
I'm hungry and I'm starving
I'm an orphan and I'm destitute
Provide for my present
And the future will provide my ambition.